Early Childhood Report Writing

Susan Louise Peterson

Early Childhood
Report Writing

Copyright

Copyright 2016 by Susan Louise Peterson

CONTENTS

Preface vii

Prologue ix

Acknowledgments xi

Introduction xiii

Chapter 1: Testing Observations 1

Chapter 2: Child Responses 21

Chapter 3: Report Writing Factors 41

Chapter 4: At-Risk Concerns 61

Chapter 5: Impact Issues 81

Index 103

Afterword 109

PREFACE

Being involved in the early childhood profession for over 25 years has let me see that children come into educational settings with a highly variable set of issues and needs. As a school psychologist and former early childhood educator, I am not diagnosing these disorders, syndromes or illnesses, but I may be involved in describing these conditions in reports or consulting with medical professionals, therapists (i.e. occupational, physical and speech therapists) and early intervention specialists who have worked with the child. There are times I am summarizing information in early childhood reports to describe the early interventions the child has received and how the child responded to those interventions. The child's background information can be really important in understanding why a child may have a delay or lack exposure to nurturing experiences and opportunities. The focus of the book *Early Childhood Report Writing* is to help professionals and college students have some examples of how the child's personal information can be described in reports that will be used in the educational setting to determine special education eligibility or additional services.

PROLOGUE

Report writing has become of great interest to me since my college days. I have always loved describing the practical side of children to see where they need help and what they are excelling in as part of their development. My first report writing book was specifically on autism. I wrote the book ***Autism Report Writing*** in 2015 because I was writing so many reports specifically on autism. However, I wanted to expand many of those ideas to broader issues related to young children with all types of needs and concerns. ***Early Childhood Report Writing*** focuses on issues for professionals and college students who see a broad array of children with different developmental delays, health issues, speech and language concerns and issues specific to the child. Each early childhood report is different and should be tailored to the unique concerns of the child.

ACKNOWLEDGMENTS

I would like to thank the many professionals who were always giving me suggestions and new ideas for early childhood report writing. I think that many professionals have such different backgrounds that it has been so helpful for me to hear professionals discuss child related issues from a medical (school nursing) perspective, a therapist perspective, a social work perspective and other educational perspectives.

A big thanks is given to my daughters as they give me a new perspective of viewing education from the personal journey that they are taking in education. My husband has always been a big support in writing and helping me with the technology aspects of writing that sometimes frustrate me as a writer. My family is wonderful an I thank each of them for their support in my writing career.

INTRODUCTION

Early childhood reports are variable in their length and style, but there is often some basic information that finds its way into most reports. Describing the child's characteristics and actions in relationship to an assessment or testing task can be combined with the child's actual responses. The area of testing observations covers a full range of engaging and communicating with the child as well as observing the child's initiation, interest and awareness during the assessment.

The child's responses during the assessment can show when a child tantrums, withdraws or is restless. As well, a child's responses may indicate uncertainty, unusual responding patterns or a wide range of sensory responses. A number of factors can be explored in the report related to illness, experience and the child's performance during the testing. A report can indicate the need for further testing and monitoring as well as when no assessments were completed.

Often young children being tested have at-risk elements and the book has a chapter exploring these at-risk concerns. These at-risk concerns can affect the child's social skills, family interactions, learning, safety, self-help skills, development and overall stability in the home and school settings. Many times at-risk factors are related to birth history and the family's background that can be related to health conditions such as allergies, surgeries, dental, vision and hearing concerns. These at-risk factors are noted in most early childhood reports.

Early Childhood Report Writing explores impact issues of how a child may be emerging or changing from intervention (or without interventions). The impact issues can look at the child's efforts, expression, limitations, cooperation and self-image. The report can explore if the child has age appropriate skills or if the child attempted tasks, took direction, comprehended tasks or needed assistance. Early childhood report writing is not an easy task at first, but once the person get the basic ideas down it is really interesting to write and describe children.

CHAPTER 1

Testing Observations

Testing observations are an important part of early childhood report writing. These observations describe the child's actions, behaviors and characteristics presented on the day of testing. The testing observations can also be described by professionals from different fields. An early childhood report may include the school psychologist's testing observations as well as the school nurses and speech therapists observations. Additional related services professionals may include their testing observations from screenings and evaluations for occupational and physical therapy, hearing and vision services. These observations all contribute to describing the child.

Varying observations can show consistent patterns of positive behavior or frustrations of the child. These testing observations may reveal changes in behavior where a child is frustrated in one part of the assessment, but more relaxed and comfortable with a different professional later in the assessment. There are different ways to phrase testing observations and some professionals are very detailed in their descriptions of the child, while other professionals are more broad and general in describing the child. This chapter focuses on some ideas for writing up testing observations for young children. Testing observations can include awareness, unsureness or even reluctant observations. A report can explore responses related to emotional and physical characteristics, language issues or even something like the location of objects.

Communication Observations

Testing observations can describe the ways the child communicates or the lack of communication the child presents in the assessment.

Examples of Communication Observations

Mark was able to express his wants and needs through words and expressions.

Mark was verbal, but his speech was difficult to understand.

Mark had difficulty following verbal directions and did not seem to understand many of the oral requests.

Mark responded well to verbal prompts and would complete tasks with a verbal cue or prompt.

Mark used no true words, but was expressive using his facial expressions and some vocal sounds.

Mark did not say any spontaneous words during the assessment, but would repeat a word on request.

Mark used no words and communicates using gestures to get his wants and needs meet.

Engagement Observations

Testing observations often point out the ease or difficulty the child had in engaging with the professionals during the assessment.

Examples of Engagement Observations

Kelly needed additional time to warm up and participate in the drawing activity, but she became focused after a few minutes.

Kelly was cooperative, but she appeared shy and reluctant to interact.

It was difficult to engage Kelly in the tasks and gain her attention.

Kelly engaged in hand posturing and would flap her hands frequently in the assessment.

Kelly would turn away and not engage or participate in the puzzle activity.

Kelly crawled under the table, moved to the corner of the room and refused to engage when give a block activity.

Kelly never engaged in any of the testing activities and refused all direct requests.

Behavior Observations

Testing observations can explore both positive behaviors and the frustration behavior of the child.

Examples of Behavior Observations

Charles played appropriately with the toys and no significant behavior concerns were observed in the session.

Charles attends a preschool and his parent did not have any behavioral concerns.

Charles was generally cooperative, but would occasionally refuse to participate if he was not interested in the task.

Charles cried often in the testing session and appeared tired.

Charles was timid, shy and very quiet throughout the assessment.

Charles had difficulty following directions and would only complete activities on his own term.

On numerous occasions, Charles would say 'no' when given a request.

Ability Observations

Testing observations can describe a child's ability levels presented in the assessment.

Examples of Ability Observations

Beth was able to match cards with broad and similar features, but had difficulty with more specific features.

Beth can stack blocks, but she had difficulty replicating a block design from a pattern.

Beth had problems placing blocks in a pattern and often had inaccurate placement of the blocks.

Beth's ability levels may be higher than tested, but due to refusal behaviors it was difficult to directly test her cognitive abilities.

Beth completed each of the matching tasks accurately and without difficulty.

Beth completed nonverbal cognitive tasks quickly and confidently, but experienced difficulty with verbal cognitive tasks.

Beth did not understand many requests and directions and appeared to be guessing or unsure of her responses.

Inconsistent Observations

Testing observations can include the child's inconsistent responses to various tasks and requests.

Examples of Inconsistent Observations

Maria was able to complete a few items when given an example, but struggled with more difficult items.

Maria could complete a one-step direction, but had difficulty with two-step directions.

Maria would not participate in verbal activities, but readily participated in nonverbal hands-on types of activities.

Maria engaged nicely in free play activities, but had a tantrum when given a structured activity.

Maria was very curious of her surroundings, but would become very upset if she was not allowed to play with her chosen toy.

Maria would participate for a few minutes and then 'shutdown' and refuse to participate in the activity.

Maria was resistant at first and then warmed up and participated in all of the activities.

Interest Observations

Testing observations can provide a broad picture of the child's interest level and participation in the assessment process.

Examples of Interest Observations

Larry would not interact or show interest in anything, but bubbles.

Larry seemed to understand all requests and showed an interest in the testing materials.

Larry showed interest in the toys with his very expressive facial expressions.

Larry only completed the block building task and lost interest to participate in any of the other testing activities.

Larry was ultra-focused on the dinosaur and would not show interest in any other toys.

Larry did not take an interest in the puzzles or blocks during free play activities and centers.

Larry was initially interested in the blocks and then became frustrated and threw them on the floor.

Initiation Observations

Testing observations can include descriptions of whether the child initiates any actions or requests to others.

Examples of Initiation Observations

Carmen did not initiate any speech and the majority of the few words she stated were not understood.

Carmen did not initiate any communication with her parents during the assessment session.

No words were spoken by Carmen in the session and she made no attempts to initiate conversations with others.

Carmen showed preference for her mother would only initiate a request from her mother.

Carmen did not initiate any interaction with nurse and refused to make eye contact or initiate a social greeting.

Carmen is starting to initiate small talk with others and her parent indicated she is making improvement in her communication skills.

Carmen often initiates a verbal request by saying 'I want that.'

Requesting Observations

Testing observations may include how the child requests or doesn't request various items or indicates a request.

Examples of Requesting Observations

Juan did not engage in any requesting or showing behaviors during the testing assessment session.

Juan requested items by pointing to the toys and no words were spoken.

Juan used gestures to request an item and then would shake his head 'yes or no' to express the desired item.

Juan is just starting to request items from his sister and other family members.

Juan used natural gestures such as nodding, shrugging his shoulders or pointing to request items.

Juan requests food items with one word responses such as 'cookie, juice or pizza.'

Juan did not show toys or point to toys of interest in the assessment and showed no requesting responses.

Redirection Observations

Testing observations may provide a picture of the child's need for redirection when requests, instructions or directions are given to him or her.

Examples of Redirection Observations

Raymond cried briefly when he did not get the toy he wanted, but was easily redirected to a new activity.

It was difficult to redirect Raymond as he was frequently glancing around the room.

Raymond had difficulty remaining attentively seated in his chair and needed redirection throughout the assessment.

It was difficult to redirect Raymond as he was fearful of many toys.

Raymond wanted to explore freely in the testing room, but was redirected to the table for an activity.

Raymond ran to the door and needed redirection back to the center activities.

Raymond needed directions repeated and did not respond well to many redirection attempts.

Play Observations

Testing observations may provide a description of how the child plays with toys, objects and others in the room.

Examples of Play Observations

Ellen would quickly become upset if she was not allowed to play with a particular toy.

Ellen did not show an interest in playing with toys as she pulled them off the shelf and tossed them on the floor.

Ellen would become stubborn if she couldn't play immediately with the toy she wanted.

Ellen played appropriately with the toys and was able to make a choice when offered two toys.

Ellen did not engage in imaginative or creative play with the toys and other children in the preschool.

Ellen responded well to an incentive to play with the toys after the table games were completed.

Ellen showed a preference for playing with the puzzle activities.

Awareness Observations

Testing observations can include the child's awareness of his or her surroundings as an important aspect in the early childhood report.

Examples of Awareness Observations

Eva had very limited interest in the testing materials, but showed awareness of some toys.

Eva seemed unaware of the group activities and was slow to complete work as she was distracted by the other preschool students.

Eva was aware where to go and found her chair with no difficulty.

Eva was unaware of what to do and she needed cues and reminders to line up for lunch.

Eva was aware of the other children and tried to reach out to them.

Eva was aware of what she needed to do and completed the task with a good effort in the preschool classroom.

Eva was aware of her surroundings and showed excitement when new toys were introduced.

Reluctant Observations

Testing observations can include children who are reluctant to participate and this behavior can be described in reports to better understand the child.

Examples of Reluctant Observations

Dirk let many therapists work with him and was not reluctant to participate.

Dirk was reluctant to come to the table and was clinging to his mother during the assessment.

Dirk was reluctant to try and stack the blocks and pushed them off of the table.

Dirk was reluctant to participate in language activities and kept walking over to the computer.

Dirk was reluctant and unresponsive to any toys that made sound or music in the preschool classroom.

Dirk was reluctant to sit in the chair as he falls easily and loses his balance.

Dirk was reluctant to transition to a new activity, but would transition with the assistance of the physical therapist.

Answering Observations

Testing observations can describe the ways the child answers questions and their responses can be varied and interesting in the report.

Examples of Answering Observations

David needed an excessive amount of reinforcement to answer the question.

David did not answer the question and it was apparent he had very limited language skills.

David did not answer verbally, but would point with nonverbal gestures.

David will need assistive technology to help him express the answer to questions in the preschool classroom.

David appears to have the ability to answer some questions, but will need adapted educational materials to support him in the Pre-Kindergarten classroom.

David was observed to have limited understanding of the concepts and cannot answer basic questions or follow simple directions.

David could not answer the questions, but assessment of his cognitive abilities should be deferred until adaptive materials are provided.

Emotional Observations

Testing observations can describe the ways the child displays emotional reactions and responses during an assessment.

Examples of Emotional Observations

Anna cried the entire assessment and appeared very sad.

Anna became upset when her friend left the preschool and she appeared very emotional.

Anna cried when her mother left her at daycare, but quickly warmed up and engaged in circle time.

Anna laughed at the funny puppet and was very engaged in the story time activity.

Anna sat very quietly and showed no emotion when presented with toys and games.

Anna smiled when the teacher praised her and gave her a sticker for following directions.

Anna appeared very serious and became upset when answered the question incorrectly.

Response Observations

Testing observations can describe the type of responding or responses the child is giving in the assessment.

Examples of Response Observations

Allen appeared to hear the sound of the toys, but did not consistently respond when his name was called.

Allen's vision screening could not be completed, but he was able to track and find the toys in the room without difficulty.

Allen was observed not to respond to his name if he was playing or engaged in an activity.

Allen's responses were limited and his eye contact was inconsistent.

Allen's response to most tasks was cooperative and he participated well in newly introduced activities.

Allen gave no response to most activities and it was difficult to engage him in new tasks.

Allen's response to visual and picture tasks was to turn away and vision concerns were noted throughout the assessment.

Physical Observations

Testing observations can describe the child's physical characteristics, responses and actions that are exhibited during the assessment.

Examples of Physical Observations

Frances was observed to have stiff finger and hand posturing throughout the assessment.

Frances was observed to play with her hair and put her hair in her mouth.

Frances became upset and was observed banging her head on the wall in the school nurse's office.

Frances was observed to have a tantrum and throw toys at her brother.

Frances spoke with a very soft voice as she whispered and mumbled words that were very difficult to recognize.

Frances was observed to pick two scabs off her hand and the nurse cleaned her hand and gave her a bandage for her hand.

Frances' body movements were observed and she appeared jerky and uncoordinated.

Language Observations

Testing observations related to language can be described in the report to identify speech and language difficulties of the child.

Examples of Language Observations

Frankie uses limited language and very few words were used in informal conversations.

Frankie's expressive language was observed to be age appropriate and on target for Kindergarten.

Frankie's nonverbal language appears appropriate, but he has a delay in his expressive language skills.

Frankie will name a few common objects, but his language and naming vocabulary is very limited.

Frankie speaks English, but has some exposure to Spanish in the home.

Frankie is developing conversation skills at a slow pace and needs help in language development.

Frankie struggles to understand language and follow oral directions in the preschool classroom.

Location Observations

Testing observations can describe the ways the child locates items or being in the appropriate location in the preschool or assessment setting.

Examples of Location Observations

James had trouble locating one item out of a small group of items.

James took his time and was visually able to locate all of the objects.

James could locate all of the large objects, but has visual difficulties with small objects.

James had difficulty locating the restroom and will need additional supervision.

James needed assistance to locate the preschool classroom and seems unsure of different locations around the school.

James does not stay with his preschool class and tends to wander to different locations in the hallway.

James stayed in the center location and followed all of his preschool teacher's directions.

CHAPTER 2

Child Responses

When a multidisciplinary team sees a child, different professionals are watching the child's responses to various people and new situations. Sometimes a child has consistent responses with various people and at other times the child responds inconsistently or differently when approached by a new person. No matter what the situation is, the professionals will be documenting the child's responses in these various settings. A report could document responses between the child and the parent during the testing situation. Communication responses describing the child's verbal and nonverbal responses can be documented in the report. Behavior responses like a child's tantrum can be noted as well as if the child is withdrawn or restless in the testing session. The report may describe if the child presents with any types of sensory responses or simply if the child has any unusual responses.

The child's confidence or uncertainty in responses can be documented in the report. Probably one of the most important responses in observing the child will be compliance responses. As professionals work with the child they will be noting if the child was compliant and cooperative or difficult and noncompliant so the team has a full picture of the child. The responses in this chapter are really important in describing the child throughout the early childhood report. The chapter furthers explores topics such as difficult, atypical and function responses along with dependent, time related, consistent, alertness and indication responses.

Verbal Responses

Different types of verbal responses are observed from the child during the assessment and these can be documented in the report communication section.

Examples of Verbal Responses

Kim did not respond verbally to the initial greeting.

Kim will repeat words, but is not using verbal indications to request items.

Kim's verbal responses are limited and she uses very few words on a daily basis.

Kim's only verbal response during the assessment was the word 'bye' on leaving the room.

Kim's verbal and expressive language skills appear age appropriate.

Kim's verbal responses and expressive language skills are limited and her speech sound system needs to be monitored once she has more words.

Kim has a strength in her verbal language skills as she uses words to express her wants, needs, thoughts and feelings.

Nonverbal Responses

Children may present a large array of nonverbal responses throughout the assessment and these responses can be included in the report.

Examples of Nonverbal Responses

John is non-verbal for the most part, but makes some vocalizations.

John imitated the nonverbal gestures for the speech therapist.

John needed a non-verbal cue and gesture to sit in the chair and participate in the assessment.

John uses gestures and nonverbal responses only and cannot verbally indicate when he is hungry or needs to request food.

John gave no nonverbal responses as he did not point to pictures in a book or gesture in the assessment.

John only nonverbally communicates by pulling his mother's hand to an object or toy.

John did not participate in nonverbal activities as he refused to point to pictures on request.

Tantrum Responses

There are some children who respond to a request with a tantrum or action that requires an explanation in the early childhood report.

Examples of Tantrum Responses

Toby had a minor tantrum when asked to participate at the table, but quickly recovered.

Toby yelled 'no' and had a refusal tantrum when a request was directed at him.

Toby had several tantrums and ignored all attempts to redirect him to new activities.

Toby had a tantrum when asked to participate and preferred to do things on his own terms.

Toby had a severe tantrum and cried for a long period of time during the nurse and speech therapy assessments.

Toby dropped to the floor and had a screaming tantrum at the beginning of the assessment.

Toby had a severe tantrum when asked a question, but later warmed up and participated in the assessment.

Withdrawn Responses

A child's withdrawn responses can be documented to describe the child's withdrawal from a request or situation.

Examples of Withdrawn Responses

Mike showed no interest in the toys and withdrew to the corner of the room.

Mike did not participate and seemed withdrawn when approached by the school nurse during the health evaluation.

Mike would turn away from a request or activity during the direct assessment activities.

Mike was withdrawn and showed very little interest in interacting with the speech therapist.

Mike was not compliant to sit at the desk and crawled under the table. His parent indicated he likes dark places.

Mike played with a few objects and then would crawl around the room and find a place under the chair.

Mike would withdraw by turning his back to the examiner when approached with an activity.

Restless Responses

A child may appear restless, overactive or fidgety during the assessment and the report can document these responses.

Examples of Restless Responses

Donna was restless and her attention span was somewhat limited.

Donna would move away from the activity as she seemed restless and distracted by the toys.

Donna turned in her seat and was restless as she would get on and off her chair frequently.

Donna was very restless when playing with toys as moved from toy to toy quickly in the room.

Donna appeared restless as she walked to the door several times and was difficult to engage in the activities.

Donna exhibited restless behavior as she did not attempt any activities and wandered the room seeking out toys of interest to her.

Donna was restless as she was fidgety in her chair and swinging her legs frequently.

Sensory Responses

In an assessment a child may exhibit sensory responses with toys and objects in the room and these can be included in the early childhood report.

Examples of Sensory Responses

Tyler was observed putting non-edible objects in his mouth and licking objects.

Tyler put a crayon in his mouth during the coloring activity.

Tyler did not avoid touching items of different textures and seemed comfortable around a variety of surfaces and fabrics.

Tyler is overly sensitive to sounds and loud noises.

Tyler turned each block around and looked intently as he carefully stacked the blocks.

Tyler will cover his ears when a toilet is flushed or music is played in the preschool classroom.

Tyler will smell each block and carefully examine it before stacking the blocks for the block activity.

Child-Parent Responses

Interactions and exchanges take place between the child and parent during the assessment and these can be documented throughout the report.

Examples of Child-Parent Responses

Billy appeared anxious and was playing with his mother's hair during the assessment.

Billy needed reassurance during the assessment and he was clingy to his mother at times.

Billy became upset and attempted to bite and hit his mother during the assessment.

Billy turned and looked at his father for reassurance and support before starting each task.

Billy would only complete the testing tasks when seated on his father's lap.

Billy needed encouragement from his mother to come to the testing table.

Billy was constantly rubbing his grandmother's arm for reassurance during the assessment.

Uncertain Responses

Children can present as confident or uncertain with their responses and these can be included in the report to check for the child's understanding of concepts.

Examples of Uncertain Responses

Mandy is uncertain what to do and does not imitate other children who are playing in her area.

Mandy would not attempt any tasks at first, but then started to gain confidence and attempted a few tasks in the assessment.

Mandy was very quick to point at pictures and there are some inconsistencies in her performance.

Mandy did not point to any pictures and seemed unsure of her responses.

Mandy was able to point and label pictures, but she struggled to answer questions.

Mandy knows a few colors and shapes, but needs to work on consistency with her preschool readiness skills and she appeared uncertain about her answers.

Mandy was unable or did not understand how to replicate block designs.

Unusual Responses

There are times when a child may respond in an unusual, different or strange way and these response can be included in the report.

Examples of Unusual Responses

Sam did not respond or look toward the door when the teacher knocked on the door three times.

Sam appeared to be ultra-focused on the toy train and did not engage with any other toys during the assessment.

Sam appears to be disconnected and standoffish when around a group of children.

Sam would toss items in the air and at other times turn them over and over in his hand.

Sam would stare at the lights in the room for long periods of time.

Sam only shows interest in one cartoon television show that is about a dog.

It was reported by Sam's mother that he is not interested in things around him and does not pay attention to what the other children are playing in preschool.

Compliance Responses

Each time a child is given a request or direction there is an observation of the child's compliance to the request and this can be described in the report.

Examples of Compliance Responses

Joe pointed to items of interest, but was not compliant to point to the requested items.

Joe was not compliant to stop hitting his brother and appeared rough in his interactions with others.

Joe did not make eye contact with the school psychologist and was not compliant to imitate or attempt any tasks.

Joe would not engage in any assessment activity and was non-compliant when approached with toys.

Joe cried throughout the assessment and was non-compliant with all requests.

Joe was very compliant and responded to each direction on first request.

Joe appeared non-compliant as he wandered the room and turned his back to the school nurse.

Difficult Responses

There are times when a child has difficulty with a task or just has a difficult time when approached with certain activities and this can be described in the report.

Examples of Difficult Responses

Mary had a difficult time remaining focused on the task and made careless mistakes.

Mary had difficulty when asked to attempt a non-preferred task and preferred to do things on her own terms.

Mary was tired in the assessment and it was difficult to gain her attention.

Mary was independent with the motor tasks and was able to move all extremities without difficulty.

Mary uses a few words, but has difficulty asking and answering questions.

Mary had difficulty when approached with any direct activity and quickly turned away.

Mary's primary difficulty is in the area of expressive language skills.

Atypical Responses

There are times a child appears atypical or a little different in the assessment session and these atypical responses can be discussed in the report.

Examples of Atypical Responses

Nick was observed to repeatedly spin the propellers on the toy airplane.

Nick visually inspected the wheels on the car and would spin the wheels for long periods of time.

Nick would often repeat words such as 'ok' or 'no way' throughout the assessment.

Nick spends most of his time lining up shoes in each closet in the house.

Nick knocked every block off of the table watching them fall to the floor.

Nick is fixated on paper as he tears pages out of books and takes the paper wrapper off of the crayons.

Nick dumped all the toys out of the box and did not show purposeful play with the toys.

Functional Responses

Assessments often look at how a child functions in a home or educational setting and the report may include comments on how the child functions in theses settings.

Examples of Functional Responses

Olivia functioned well in a new environment and quickly engaged in the circle time activity.

Olivia's strength was determined by observing her functional mobility and play skills.

Olivia demonstrated global delays and will require adaptations and modifications to function and access materials in the school environment.

Olivia appears to function with age appropriate speech and language skills and was exited from speech services.

Olivia's adaptive functioning was in the average range when compared to same age peers.

Olivia is not consistently using words to communicate in a functional manner.

Olivia will need speech and language services to address her functional communication delays.

Dependent Responses

Some children are dependent for help or assistance and these dependent responses can be described in the report.

Examples of Dependent Responses

Ryan has difficulty with transfers and is dependent on adult assistance with all transfer activities.

Ryan is dependent on adult assistance for all mobility activities.

Ryan needs constant supervision and maximal adult assistance with accessing educational materials in the classroom.

Ryan has difficulty with self-care tasks and dependent for help with all hygiene activities.

Ryan has limited upright head control, but is dependent on assistance from others.

Ryan is very dependent on adult supervision to help with adaptive equipment in the school environment.

Ryan falls frequently and is dependent on adults to safely move around the educational setting.

Time Responses

Children may need more time to complete tasks or have time related issues that can be described in various sections of the early childhood report.

Examples of Time Responses

Erik was able to engage in activities and his attention was sustained for a lengthy period of time.

Erik's parent indicated he needs additional time to transition off of the playground and during safety drills.

Erik needs more time to visually locate items on the floor.

Erik will reach for items, but needs extra time to coordinate hand and arm movements.

Erik fatigues easily and may need time to rest after movement activities.

Erik may need a short break and more time during intensive visual tasks.

Erik requires extended time to process directions and requests.

Consistent Responses

It is important to note in the report when a child is giving consistent responses or responding in a consistent way.

Examples of Consistent Responses

Tim was able to consistently follow oral directions without gestural cues.

Tim consistently demonstrated the ability to walk, run, climb and jump off objects.

Tim consistently used a pointing response and had no difficulty pointing on request.

Tim made consistent and appropriate eye contact throughout the assessment.

Tim consistently responded to his name when asked to attempt tasks in the assessment.

Tim's mother reported that he interacts with other children on a consistent basis at his preschool.

Tim consistently completed all tasks and followed each direction on first request.

Alertness Responses

The early childhood report may include statements that describe the child's alertness to objects, people and the environment.

Examples of Alertness Responses

Cindy showed alertness and turned her head when her father's cell phone rang during the assessment.

Cindy briefly showed alertness and opened her eyes when a flashing light was moved in front of her face.

Cindy turned her head to the right and showed alertness to the musical toy.

Cindy was alert and aware as she was able to follow a visual pattern on the computer screen.

Cindy was alert and able to follow a visual pattern with colorful items.

Cindy shows some alertness of her environment as she tries to look out of the car window.

Cindy is alerted by moving objects and shows a preference for movement types of toys.

Indication Responses

A child may use certain actions to indicate the need for an object or demonstrate an attempt to communicate or show an emotion and this can be included in the report.

Examples of Indication Responses

Cody was able to turn his head to the left indicating he was hearing the bell on the left side.

Cody was able to indicate an awareness of an object that was placed in his hand for a short duration.

Cody will scoot himself forward to indicate interest in an object.

Cody will indicate pleasure or enjoyment by briefly smiling when a musical toy is placed near him.

Cody was able to move his head up and down to indicate that he could follow the movement of the light.

Cody makes a facial expression to indicate when he is unhappy with something.

Cody indicates listening by looking toward his mother's face when she speaks and sings to him.

CHAPTER 3

Report Writing Factors

There are many factors that reports can address when explaining the complexities of the assessment, differing opinions and how the child is related by the parent. For instance, professionals can have differences from various training experiences and sometimes these different perspectives need to be discussed in a report. Illness and anxiety factors are important in describing the child's health in the report. Many children have a variety of services from agencies and these services can be described in the report. Documentation can be included in a report to describe the child's performance and the varying levels of experience that the child has had in the home and outside of the home. The child's experiences can be explained in the report to understand the child.

An early childhood report can include an explanation of the need for further monitoring or further testing that is warranted as the child develops or gains more experiences. The report could explore if assessments cannot be conducted or if undetermined factors need to be explained. A variety of other factors in the report could be related to the child's avoidance behaviors, frustration, struggles, facial expression, health and general participation during the assessment. Often a report will focus on the child's weaknesses and strengths to get a full picture of the child and to help the professionals and parents make important decisions regarding the child's future educational programs or possibilities.

Illness Factors

Illness, injury, health and medical factors can be reviewed and discussed in the early childhood report.

Examples of Illness Factors

Janet has a history of a near drowning accident, but appears to have made a wonderful recovery and is responding well to interventions.

Janet's accident resulted in a traumatic brain injury that will impact her learning.

Janet has received cancer treatment and it is unclear how it will impact her educational progress.

Janet's progress will need to be monitored closely after her next surgery.

Janet has a history of failure to thrive and feeding issues were noted by the occupational therapist.

Janet's medical records were reviewed and she is cleared to attend school and participate in activities as tolerated.

Janet has had hip surgery and will be attending school in a cast and transported in a manual wheelchair.

Anxiety Factors

The child's may appear anxious or have some worrisome types of behaviors and these can be described in the early childhood report.

Examples of Anxiety Factors

Phillip was observed to bite his nails and put his fingers in his mouth during the assessment.

Phillip needed reassurance and looked often at his mother during the assessment and testing session.

Phillip cried and screamed when his brother turned the lights out.

Phillip paced back and forth when his dad left the room for a few minutes.

Phillip was uncomfortable and worrisome when he made a mistake and tended to feel uncomfortable when the answer was not correct.

Phillip was clingy to his mother when the family entered the testing room.

Phillip appeared nervous as he was swinging his legs in the chair.

Agency Service Factors

If a child has received services from various agencies it is important to document these services in the early childhood report.

Examples of Agency Service Factors

Molly's caseworker noted that she has had multiple foster care placements in the past six months.

The early intervention service documented that Molly's family actively participated in all intervention sessions.

Molly's mother stopped early intervention services after only a few months due to her work schedule.

Molly was hospitalized and unable to participate in early intervention services for three months.

Molly's family went on vacation for a month to Mexico and intervention services were interrupted.

Molly was referred by child protective services for an early childhood assessment.

Molly was referred to a school medical clinic for additional health related concerns by a school nurse.

Performance Factors

The child's performance during the assessment can be described in the report and contribute to making placement and eligibility decisions.

Examples of Performance Factors

Alex attempted most tasks presented to him with a moderate level of praise.

Alex would only complete a task when given an oral direction combined with a prompt.

Alex needed an example in order to complete a task and was unable to understand the task without an example.

Alex completed all tasks quickly and seemed to have a good understanding of preschool readiness tasks.

Alex's intervention specialist noted that he achieved all developmental milestones at expected ages.

Alex played around in some activities as if guessing some answers wrong at first and then picking the correct response.

Alex changed his answer and self-corrected during the testing.

Description Factors

Reports can include some descriptions of the child's appearance and presentation during the assessment process.

Examples of Description Factors

Julia had a red skin reaction from a band aid and may be allergic to latex.

Julia's eyes frequently rolled upward and inward so a vision assessment was requested.

Julia was appropriately groomed and casually dressed during the assessment.

Julia presented as a happy, friendly little girl who was curious and interested in toys.

Julia has a cold and the assessment was stopped as she appeared sick and very tired.

Julia had a frown on her face and appeared sad throughout the entire assessment.

Julia had a clump of missing fair and her mother shared that she cut her own hair.

Experience Factors

Children have a wide variety of experiences in the home, childcare settings or outside of the home and these experiences can be described in the reports.

Examples of Experience Factors

Clay was unable to attend preschool due to an immune disorder and has had no interaction with other children outside of the home.

Clay has had limited play experiences outside of the home and only plays with his brother in the home.

Clay has not been exposed to a daycare or preschool.

Clay's mother indicated that she picks up the toys and that Clay has had no clean up experience.

Clay has no experiences using eating utensils and his father noted that he feeds him.

Clay socializes well with other children and has had many play experiences at preschool, the church nursery and the children's gym class.

Clay received early intervention for two years and has made tremendous gains as he has reached all developmental milestones.

Further Testing Factors

A report may emphasize the need for the child to have further testing or a delay for further testing and this can be described in the report.

Examples of Further Testing Factors

Mick's phonological assessment should be completed once he gains more vocabulary skills.

An additional cognitive assessment should be considered for Mick once he gains more words.

Mick's parents had concerns related to Mick's use of stairs so a physical therapy assessment is recommended in the school setting.

An occupational therapy assessment was initiated to address Mick's sensory issues.

Mick will need further testing in the area of comprehension and understanding since he only had limited participation in the initial assessment.

Mick's language assessment was a minimal estimation of his skills and he will need further testing since he did not participate in the direct assessment.

As Mick's skills emerge and he has more preschool experiences further testing would be helpful to get a picture of his abilities and skills.

Monitoring Factors

There are some evaluations and assessments on young children that suggest monitoring the child's progress or actions from early childhood experiences.

Examples of Monitoring Factors

Jim's cognitive abilities should be monitored once he has gained more preschool experiences.

Jim's adaptive skills should be observed and monitored in the preschool setting.

The school site should continue to monitor the need for a possible occupational therapy assessment in the preschool setting.

Jim was resistive in the testing and his academic progress should be monitored throughout the school year.

Continue to monitor Jim's social development and inform the school site of any behavioral issues or related treatments.

Jim's expressive language skills should be monitored as he acquires more language experiences and learning to learn behaviors.

Jim's behavior should be monitored to see if there is a need for a behavior plan in the school setting.

No Assessment Factors

There are times when assessments cannot be conducted or there is not need for an assessment and these factors can be described in the report.

Examples of No Assessment Factors

Mary had a tantrum and no direct assessments were completed due to her behavior.

Mary said 'no' to all requests and not direct assessment was completed due to refusal behaviors.

Mary had a short attention span so no formal assessments were completed.

Mary's speech sound skills were not tested due to her limited vocabulary.

Mary's speech assessment could not be completed because she had difficulty with imitation and labeling activities.

Mary did not participate in the direct assessment so an interview and observation were utilized to complete the assessment.

Mary's current assessment results should be reviewed with caution due to second language issues that may not reflect her full potential.

Undetermined Factors

There are times when situations or disorders may not show the complete picture of the child and these factors can be explained in the report.

Examples of Undetermined Factors

At this time, it cannot be determined if Lane's cerebral palsy will adversely impact him educationally.

Lane's mother reported sensory concerns, but no sensory characteristics were observed in the assessment so sensory concerns should be monitored at the school.

Lane's motor concerns could possibly impact his ability to participate and move safety in the school setting.

It is unclear how Lane's six ear infections have impacted his speech and language skills.

Lane did not participate in the assessment so an estimations of his level of communication was obtained from parent interview and observations.

Lane's difficulty with balance and coordination may impact his independence and require supervision.

Lane's low tone and motor weakness may impact his access to educational materials and transitions in the school setting.

Avoidance Factors

There are children who will do various things in the assessment to show avoidance of interacting with people or objects and these can be included in the reports.

Examples of Avoidance Factors

Brett made no eye contact and turned away to avoid any interaction with the school nurse.

Brett avoided the testing by crawling under a chair and turning away from the school psychologist.

Brett avoided all tasks by standing in the corner with his back to the examiner.

Brett completed no tasks and avoided all attempts to directly participate in the assessment.

Brett refused to get off of the floor, avoided all tasks and would not approach the activity table.

Brett put his coat over his head to cover his face and avoid working with the speech therapist.

Brett turned over and remained face down on the floor to avoid the requests and directions.

Frustration Factors

A child's frustration is often described in the report because it frequently impacts the assessment and the child's ability to participate in the testing.

Examples of Frustration Factors

Sam became very frustrated when he could not get the toy open.

Sam had a tantrum immediately after he became frustrated with a task that was difficult.

Sam quickly became frustrated when oral tasks were presented, but was calm when working on nonverbal tasks.

Sam showed frustration by shouting 'no' and shaking his head at the request.

Sam appeared stubborn and strong willed when he became frustrated with the tasks that were presented to him.

Sam will quickly bite other children when he is frustrated and does not get his way.

Sam was frustrated at first, but calmed down once he warmed up to the testing room.

Struggle Factors

A child may struggle to complete a task or understand a concept and a report can include examples of these struggles.

Examples of Struggle Factors

Steve pushed away all picture books and struggled with visual activities.

Steve struggled to describe objects, but was able to say a few single words.

Steve only pointed to objects and struggled to make any kind of verbal request.

Steve's parent indicated that his is very aggressive and struggles with behavior in the home setting.

Steve cried when his dad left the room and he struggled with separation.

Steve was clingy to his mother and struggled to let go of his mother and come to the table.

Steve had acting-out behaviors and struggled with his ability to express himself.

Facial Expression Factors

A report may often describe a child's facial expressions or how the child responds to facial expressions usually as a communication or social skills component.

Examples of Facial Expression Factors

Marsha did not respond to her mother's facial expression or make any attempt to communicate with her mother.

Marsha smiled when her father entered the room and she seemed delighted to see him.

Marsha appeared sad when her mother told her 'no' and gave her a frowning facial expression.

Marsha stuck her tongue out as she refused the tasks presented by the school psychologist.

Marsha would close her eyes and avoid any eye contact or facial expression when approached with tasks.

Marsha pouted throughout the whole assessment indicating frustration in her facial expression.

Marsha had a friendly facial expression and smiled frequently to indicate pleasure with the activities.

Health Factors

Early childhood reports often discuss a broad range of general health factors that may or may not impact the child's development.

Examples of Health Factors

Brent's appetite varies and he is a very picky eater.

Brent's seizures could impact him in the school setting and a seizure alert has been placed in the school file.

Brent is healthy and has no major health problems or issues that will impact his education.

Brent appeared small and his growth needs to be monitored as he attends preschool.

Brent had four surgeries in his first year of life, but all problem areas have been resolved and there are no current health concerns.

Brent is healthy and has no health or physical limitations.

Brent refused many of the vision and hearing screening requests during the health assessments.

Participation Factors

A child may show varying levels of participation throughout the assessment process and this can be presented in the report.

Examples of Participation Factors

Joan has difficulty with her moods and can become easily upset when participating in preschool activities.

Joan would only participate when standing by her father and refused to come to the table.

Joan's participation changed quickly when she didn't get her desired object and hit her mother.

Joan willingly entered the room and came to the table quickly to participate.

Joan participates and performs tasks only when it is on her own terms.

Joan only participates in non-verbal tasks and avoided participating in all verbal tasks.

Joan would not participate or acknowledge any of the other children in the preschool classroom.

Weakness Factors

The areas of weakness or where the child has delays can be discussed in the report to explain where the child needs help or assistance.

Examples of Weakness Factors

Rita struggles with sharing toys and has a weakness with turn taking activities.

Rita has a weakness in her ability to orally communicate with other children in the preschool classroom.

Rita has a weakness in the play area and does not engage in purposeful or interactive play with other children.

Rita has a weakness in transitions and struggles with any change in routine.

Rita has a weakness in her daily living skills and has difficulty with toileting, dressing, eating and safety.

Rita has a weakness in her gross motor skills as she struggles with running, throwing and catching objects.

Rita's nonverbal cognitive abilities are in the average range, but she has a weakness in her verbal cognitive abilities.

Strength Factors

The report can describe a short summary, statement or comment of the child's strengths throughout the various sections of the report.

Examples of Strength Factors

Angie's strength in the area of conversational speech appeared to be adequate for the preschool setting and no delays were noted.

Angie's strength is in her ability to be very cooperative, attentive and easy to work with in the preschool classroom.

Angie has a strength in understanding language and her receptive language skills are average when compared to same age peers.

Angie has strong motor skills and is able to complete motor tasks with ease.

Angie has a strength in her socialization skills as she plays cooperatively with other children and gets along well in group activities.

Angie's strong cognitive abilities were apparent as she did not get upset if a task was challenging.

Angie's daily living skills are strong as she is toilet trained and dresses herself with minimal assistance.

CHAPTER 4

At-Risk Concerns

At-risk concerns are often noted throughout early childhood reports. Since some child are from at-risk family situations certain concerns can be noted. Review of medical histories will often describe concerns of the child, family and extended family members. Behavioral histories may note mental health concerns, mental hospitalizations and disorders that may possibly impact the child in the future. As well, learning and cognitive abilities can be noted from the family history and the child's preschool readiness experiences. Social and related concerns may note at-risk factors such as prison, foster care or separation from families that impact young children presently and in the future years.

Although many factors can be discussed as at-risk concerns these factors are usually pointed back to describing the child's present situation with notes about possibilities that may impact the child's educational situation. Early childhood assessment reports often focus on describing the child's health background, medical concerns, behavioral and social issues, the family situation and the early childhood learning experiences of the child. A description of these at-risk concerns can often indicate to professionals some 'red flags' or warnings that may need to be considered if problems are noted in the child's behavior, growth, health, family or educational situations. The report can explore at-risk concerns related to everyday dressing as well as pragmatic or practical issues. Certainly concerns related to the child's background, birth history, developmental issues, allergy concerns, dental issues and surgeries can be discussed and that may make the child at-risk for various future conditions.

Social At-Risk Concerns

There are times a child may be behaving in a particular way because of a variety social concerns that impact educational experiences and are reported.

Examples of Social At-Risk Concerns

Cory has been exposed to domestic violence and is at-risk for behavioral issues.

Cory was emotionally abused by his previous foster family and is at risk for emotional concerns and possible counseling.

Cory has been exposed to physical abuse and his aggressive behaviors toward others must be monitored.

Cory was in protective custody due to criminal activity in the home and is at-risk for social and emotional concerns.

Cory has experienced prenatal drug exposure and has been treated for drug dependency.

Cory has been exposed to inappropriate language and mom indicated that he uses obscene language.

Cory has no contact with father who is incarcerated.

Family At-Risk Concerns

Family at-risk concerns can have a strong impact on a child's development and can be discussed in the report to give a detailed picture of the child.

Examples of Family At-Risk Concerns

Van's father was a sperm donor and the family medical history of the father is not known.

Van's parents have split custody and he stays with each parent several days a week.

Van's household includes his mother and younger brother and he has no contact with his father.

Van's parent reported behavioral and emotional concerns on both sides of the family medical history.

Van's parents are currently dealing with family court to determine custody and where Van will reside during the week.

Van's grandmother is unsure of his birth history and developmental milestones.

Van's family has had frequent moves, but appears to have more stability with dad's new job and an improved housing situation.

Unstable At-Risk Concerns

Unstable at-risk concerns may be related to changing family schedules, flexible work hours or frequent moves that impact the child's sense of security.

Examples of Unstable At-Risk Concerns

Ginger has regressed in her development from moving to three different states in the last six months.

Ginger has a history of frequent moves between her grandparents and parents homes that may impact her behavior.

Ginger's mother works a split shift at the hospital so the family has irregular sleep times.

Ginger appeared anxious when her stepfather arrived at the assessment and she ran to her mother.

Ginger was placed in foster care recently and appears to be sad and withdrawn.

Ginger is a twin and lives between two households as her parents are separated and dealing with custody issues.

Ginger was taken out of early intervention services due to mom's work schedule and only received a few weeks of early intervention.

Safety At-Risk Concerns

A report may include a description of safety concerns for the child and let professionals know the areas a child may need more supervision.

Examples of Safety At-Risk Concerns

Ben is at-risk for safety issues as he is a runner and unaware of sidewalk safety.

Ben climbed on the table twice during the assessment and is at risk for safety concerns related to furniture utilization.

Ben is at-risk for bus safety concerns related to accessing the bus stairs.

Ben will run in traffic and needs close adult supervision for safety issues.

Ben is unaware of common dangers and at-risk for safety injuries as he jumps off high playground equipment.

Ben is at-risk for falling on uneven surfaces due to his poor coordination.

Ben will attempt to go to unsafe situations and needs very close supervision due to his extremely poor safety awareness.

Learning At-Risk Concerns

The early childhood assessment report may focus on the child's learning abilities and preschool readiness skills.

Examples of Learning At-Risk Concerns

Throughout the assessment, Candy displayed difficulties in understanding directions and is at-risk for learning problems.

Candy has a diagnosis of Down Syndrome which puts her at-risk for an intellectual disability.

Candy has yet to understand matching concepts and picture identification even though she has had early intervention services.

Candy would hurry through the assessment tasks and she often made careless errors.

Candy has had no early interventions or preschool and appears to struggle with learning new concepts.

Candy is at-risk for learning problems as she did not complete some cognitive testing and did not respond to many verbal requests and directions.

Candy had difficulty with learning tasks and directions had to be repeated and modeled for her

Vision At-Risk Concerns

During the assessment process professionals may note vision concerns related to vision history, glasses or eye surgery that can be documented in the reports.

Examples of Vision At-Risk Concerns

Brett does not wear his prescribed glasses and is at-risk for vision difficulties in the classroom.

Brett turns away from visual tasks and appears to have visual tracking issues when looking at pictures.

Brett does not wear his glasses as they are broken and new glasses have not been obtained due to insurance issues.

Brett's parents had vision concerns and a referral was made to vision services.

Brett did not attempt the visual tasks of matching pictures and pointing to the dots on the card.

Brett's test scores should be reviewed with caution as the parents mentioned vision concerns later in the assessment.

Brett does not meet the criteria for eligibility as a child with a vision impairment, but may receive some vision accommodations for the school environment.

Hearing At-Risk Concerns

Hearing concerns related to ear infections, hearing aids, ear surgeries and general hearing issues can be described in the early childhood report.

Examples of Hearing At-Risk Concerns

Amy is at-risk for hearing concerns due to a significant family history of hearing problems.

Amy spoke loudly and an audio referral was issued.

Amy did not respond to her name, but her parents had no concerns as she recently passed a hearing test.

Amy was inconsistent in her responses as she did not respond to her name, but was alerted by the sound of the toys.

Amy has a history of ear infections and is at-risk of hearing concerns.

Amy did not complete the hearing screening and did not tolerate anything near her ears as she took the headset off.

Amy's parents had no hearing concerns, but a hearing referral was issued by the school nurse.

Motor At-Risk Concerns

Motor concerns can be documented in the report to explain the child's motor capabilities and ability to get around a school campus.

Examples of Motor At-Risk Concerns

Jacob has received physical therapy in the past, but appeared study and independent on his feet in the health assessment.

Jacob's muscle strength and tone appeared adequate, but he presented as being slightly uncoordinated.

Jacob had purposeful movements, but sometimes lost his balance.

Jacob's gross motor skills should be monitored as he has difficulty kicking a ball and jumping up and down.

Jacob held the pencil with a fisted grasp and was unable to copy designs from a demonstration.

Jacob puts his knees on the chair and his motor movements were somewhat awkward.

Jacob's low muscle tone has adversely impacted his gross motor skills, but he is making progress.

Eating At-Risk Concerns

There are times children have concerns in the areas of eating and feeding and these considerations and issues can be described in the report.

Examples of Eating At-Risk Concerns

Marvin has a history of feeding problems that will need to be monitored in preschool.

Marvin was diagnosed with feeding problems as an infant and continues to receive g-tube feedings.

There are no current feeding concerns and Marvin's g-tube is scheduled to be removed next month.

Marvin is a very picky eater and tends to under eat.

Marvin's parent had no early eating concerns, but now has concerns related to chewing and swallowing foods.

Marvin has food allergies to peanuts and nuts and a food allergy alert was initiated for the school.

Marvin often overstuffs his mouth and needs supervision as he is at-risk for gagging.

Medical At-Risk Concerns

Medical issues and conditions for the child can be described in the report in order to show understanding of risk concerns for the child.

Examples of Medical At-Risk Concerns

Kate gets infections easily and her immune system is reported to be at-risk.

Kate has a significant medical history and multiple surgeries that may impact her in the school setting.

Although Kate had some early health concerns, her general health is good and she takes no medications.

Kate's early injury puts her at-risk for global developmental delays that will adversely impact her educationally.

Kate has cerebral palsy and dependent on adult assistance with all daily living and motor activities.

Kate was born pre-mature and is at-risk for delays and health related concerns.

Kate has delays and received speech and occupational therapy while overseas for her mother's military service.

Surgery At-Risk Concerns

Often young children have had surgeries that contribute to at-risk concerns related to their health and development and these can be described in the report.

Examples of Surgery At-Risk Concerns

Dale has a history of seizures, but no surgery is recommended at this time.

Dale is followed by a variety of medical specialists and several surgeries are scheduled in the coming months.

Dale has had previous ear infections and just had surgery for ear tube placements this spring.

Dale has had two laser surgeries on his left eye and needs to wear glasses for eye protection.

Dale was sick as an infant, but there is no documentation of serious injuries or surgeries.

Dale has had heart surgery as an infant and was kept in the hospital for four weeks to grow after the surgery.

Dale has some scarring on his chest from previous cardiac surgeries.

Dressing At-Risk Concerns

Some children have dressing concerns and the child's independence or need for assistance with dressing tasks can be described in the report.

Examples of Dressing At-Risk Concerns

Chad will take off his diaper to indicate when soiled, but is still learning to ask for help.

Chad has difficulty putting on a shirt and often needs help as he is at-risk of losing his balance.

Chad is not putting on clothes independently and needs an example and encouragement to get dressed.

Chad needs assistance with dressing as he has left side weakness.

Chad can remove all of his clothes, but needs assistance with putting on clothing.

Chad needs to be assisted with dressing, but will hold his arms out to help with dressing.

Chad can partially put on pants, but needs assistance as he has difficulty pulling clothing upward.

Pragmatic At-Risk Concerns

Reports may include ideas related to pragmatic or practical ways the child communicates with others.

Examples of Pragmatic At-Risk Concerns

Della has delayed language skills and is at-risk for difficulties with pragmatic skills in social contexts.

Della is starting to smile and point to things as her pragmatic skills are improving.

Della's pragmatic language delays will have an adverse social, emotional and academic effect.

Della is emerging in her pragmatic non-verbal exchanges of waving and taking turns.

Della is not using pragmatic skills like gesturing, shaking her head or tapping another child to gain attention.

Della was observed to use pragmatic skills as she gave a toy to another child and reached out to accept a toy.

Della was observed to make many social attempts to reach out to other children and her pragmatic skills appear age appropriate.

Background At-Risk Concerns

The early childhood report can include a discussion of the child's background concerns that may impact the child's development.

Examples of Background At-Risk Concerns

Karli's foster parent expressed concerns regarding fetal alcohol syndrome due to her mother's use of drugs and alcohol during pregnancy.

Karli's family medical history reported heart disease and hypertension on the father's side.

Karli's family background includes speech and language problems on both her mother's and father's side.

Karli's mother began pre-natal care the first month of pregnancy and took prenatal vitamins.

Karli has been exposed to domestic violence and abuse at around 2 years of age.

Karli's family medical history on her mother's side includes depression and an anxiety disorder.

Karli's mother had severe vomiting throughout the pregnancy and was treated with medication.

Birth At-Risk Concerns

A child's birth history may reveal at-risk concerns and this information is often included in the health assessment or school nurse section of the report.

Examples of Birth At-Risk Concerns

Carrie weighed eight pounds and it was reported that a cord was wrapped around her neck and oxygen was administered.

Carrie's birth weight was 6lbs 3oz and no perinatal complications were noted.

Carrie had a significant birth history including being born at 25 weeks and spending months in the hospital.

Carrie passed the newborn hearing screening and was discharged home with mom and dad.

Carrie was born with a hospital vaginal delivery and not complications were reported.

Carrie was a c-section delivery due to fetal heart distress and pregnancy complications.

Carrie's birth information was obtained from parent interviews and a review of the health form.

Developmental At-Risk Concerns

Early childhood reports for the most part do a good job in discussing the child's developmental history.

Examples of Developmental At-Risk Concerns

Sue's developmental history noted failure to thrive and numerous eating problems.

Sue's developmental language delay interferes with her ability to communicate and express herself.

Sue's developmental history and awkward movements were discussed with parent as well as the potential benefit of a genetic evaluation.

Sue's global delays adversely impact her development and special education services are recommended.

Sue's parents have developmental concerns related to her motor skills and balance.

Sue appears small and the nurse recommended the school site nurse monitor her growth and development.

Sue's parents have developmental concerns about her social skills and her aggressive behaviors have become more of an issue.

Allergy At-Risk Concerns

It is not uncommon for allergies to be discussed in early childhood reports and how they impact the child.

Examples of Allergy At-Risk Concerns

Van broke out in hives after eating strawberries and his mother thinks it is an allergic reaction.

Van is sensitive to the protein in milk and an alert for allergy to milk protein was initiated by the school nurse.

Van has no food allergies and seems to tolerate all types of food, but has a latex allergy.

Van tested positive for an allergy to dog dander and the dog allergy alert will be sent to the appropriate school staff.

Van is allergic to soy and it irritates his stomach and must be avoided.

Van is healthy for the most part, but suffers with seasonal allergies.

Van is allergic to fish and presently does not have an epi-pen.

Dental At-Risk Concerns

There are child who present with challenging dental related concerns that can be noted in the report.

Examples of Dental At-Risk Concerns

Joey did not open his mouth on request for the oral examination.

Joey's teeth were free of decay for the most part, but the nurse noted tarter on his back teeth.

Joey's gums and teeth appeared healthy at a glance during the nurse's screening.

Joey has never been to a dentist and has not had a dental exam.

Joey has discolored teeth, but no obvious decay was noted on a visual observation.

Joey was born with a left sided cleft lip that required oral surgery to close the cleft palate.

Joey has not medical or dental problems related to chewing or swallowing.

CHAPTER 5

Impact Issues

There are a number of issues that impact children and these issues can be described in early childhood reports. The reports can certainly describe a child's emerging skills and improvement in completing activities. How a child changes and behaves during the assessment can be explored as well as the amount of effort the child gives and whether the child is at an age appropriate level. The report can focus on how the child expresses him or herself and self-confidence issues related to how the child views him or herself. There can be a discussion of the child's limitations and if intensive services are required or if consultation with other professionals should be considered. Certainly a report can discuss the child's cooperation during the assessment session that give a picture of description of how the child works with others.

The report may explore what tasks the child attempts as well as the child's comprehension related to those tasks. A report may discuss if the child seemed to understand the task or was just guessing some of the responses. The report can describe how the child follows directions and demonstrates what he or she can do. The child's habits can be explored and social exchanges or lack of social interaction can be discussed in the report. Some children will need more assistance and children with significant delays can be explained in the report as these children may need more substantial support in the educational setting.

Emerging Issues

Early childhood reports can discuss skills that the child is emerging in or showing some improvement of development.

Examples of Emerging Issues

Jay has displayed emerging skills in his ability to use words and social greetings with others.

Jay is starting to use words to express desired objects and seems to be emerging in his ability to request objects.

Jay has received physical therapy and his parent commented that he is emerging in his ability to stand and take a few steps.

Jay is responding well to early intervention services and his preschool readiness skills have emerged.

Jay has made significant gains from intervention and presents with many emerging skills.

Jay's emerging language skills can be supported through a preschool program.

Jay's emerging socialization skills will be enhanced through small group instruction.

Change Issues

There are times when a child's behavior or actions changes during the assessment and this can be documented in the report.

Examples of Change Issues

Sandy did not want to sit down for tasks initially, but with encouragement from her mother she came to the table and completed most activities.

Sandy was shy at first and then warmed up and became more interactive in the testing session.

Sandy participated at first and then became distracted by the toys.

Sandy only participated for a brief period of time and then abruptly said 'no' to all requests and directions.

Sandy did not make eye contact at first, but when the toys were presented she made eye contact and actively participated in the play experience.

Sandy had difficulty complying with directions, but when given redirection she was able to comply with basic instructions.

Sandy had many refusal behaviors, but finally participated when given verbal reinforcement and praise.

Effort Issues

Early childhood reports may describe the child's effort when attempting or completing tasks.

Examples of Effort Issues

Noah actively participated in the assessment and made a sincere effort on each task.

Noah's effort was limited and he needed constant reminders to return to his seat.

Noah made no effort to participate in any of the testing activities so parent report and observations were used to obtain information during the assessment.

Noah put forth a good effort during the testing and attempted all tasks.

Noah tried his best and gave an appropriate effort when working one on one with the speech therapist.

It was difficult to determine Noah's true effort and performance as he had many refusal behaviors and limited participation.

Noah's effort was minimal as he preferred to do activities on his own terms.

Age Appropriate Issues

There are times professionals may relate the child's performance to that of age appropriate levels and this can be discussed in reports.

Examples of Age Appropriate Issues

Bryan does not have age appropriate words in his vocabulary and only makes a few sounds during the assessment.

When compared to age appropriate peers, Bryan's daily living skills were in the below average range.

Bryan struggles with motor skills and is in the low range in comparison with same age peers.

Bryan has difficulty expressing his wants and needs at an age appropriate level.

Bryan's cognitive abilities appear age appropriate and within age level expectancies.

Bryan's use of language was less than what is expected in view of his chronological age.

Bryan demonstrated age appropriate expressive language skills and vocal quality.

Expression Issues

The early childhood report may include a description of the way a child is expressing him or herself through requests and responses.

Examples of Expression Issues

Victor expressed himself and tried to get his father's attention by hitting the desk and banging toys on the desk.

Victor had a limited range of facial expression and only smiled once during the assessment.

Victor's expressive language skills are emerging and he is starting to speak more at preschool.

Victor expresses himself by reaching for or pointing to a desired object.

Victor banged blocks together and threw blocks at the wall communicate and express himself.

Victor gestured to his parents to communicate and express his interest in the new toy.

Victor responded to his mother's facial expression and appeared to recognize her as a caregiver.

Self Issues

There are times the early childhood report may include ideas about how the child views him or herself in relation to others.

Examples of Self Issues

Kay does not seem to understand showing concern for others and seldom makes contact with other children.

Kay responded to her face in the mirror and smiled when the mirror was close to her.

Kay frequently said 'I'm done' and refused to attempt any tasks.

Kay will not completed most tasks by herself unless she has an excessive amount of praise and reinforcement.

Kay is cooperative, compliant and presents as having the ability to relate well to others in the preschool setting.

Kay does not follow directions well and she often needs an example and the directions to be repeated.

Kay will attempt most tasks, but gets frustrated quickly when she is unable to complete a task.

Limitation Issues

A report can describe how the child may have some limitations that impact his or her development or performance in an educational setting.

Examples of Limitation Issues

Jose had received no direct services and has had very limited early childhood learning experiences.

Jose has motor limitations and his teacher may want to consider a computer assisted program.

Jose is a second language learner and has had limited exposure to English.

Jose is being referred to a speech therapist as he has limited vocabulary in both English and Spanish.

Jose has had limited exposure to books and his parent is encourage to help him explore Kindergarten level books at the school and public library.

Jose has vision limitations and the Pre-kindergarten teacher should consider a seating arrangement close to the instructional boards.

Jose has hearing limitations and teaching materials should use more than one sense (i.e. hearing, seeing, touching etc.)

Intensive Issues

Some children will need more intensive services, instruction or interventions as they have more severe delays or needs and this can be discussed in the report.

Examples of Intensive Issues

Shane continues to have a high frequency of inattentive behaviors at preschool and requires intensive one-to-one instruction.

Shane needs one-to-one assistance as he has intensive levels of anxiety and stress in the preschool setting.

Shane needs more intensive preschool instruction as previous early childhood interventions have not worked well.

Shane is extremely aggressive as he often hits other children in Kindergarten and an intensive behavior specialist is recommended.

Shane needs intensive preschool instruction as he has extremely low comprehension and cognitive abilities.

Shane does not retain Kindergarten information well and will need more intensive instruction for the next year.

Shane needs a more intensive preschool setting as he struggles with behavior and has not responded well to early intervention services.

Consultation Issues

An early childhood report may mention or focus on consultation issues related to the child's development.

Examples of Consultation Issues

Luke's parents may want to consult with the regional center for support related to intellectual disabilities.

Luke has motor limitations and consultation with the assistive technology department is recommended.

Luke's parents may want to consult with the computer center about checking out a computer to practice preschool readiness skills.

Luke's family may want to consult with a local autism organization to find family group support and resources.

Luke enjoys sports and his parents may want to consult with a local adaptive physical education sports program.

Luke's family should consider consulting with the local community recreation center for enrichment activities.

Luke's family may want to consider an after school program to provide activities for social interaction.

Cooperation Issues

Report will often discuss or describe how the child cooperates in the testing tasks and requests during testing.

Examples of Cooperation Issues

Austin was very cooperative and attentive throughout the entire assessment.

Austin was uncooperative and did not attempt any tasks during the assessment.

Austin started to cry and had limited cooperation as could not be engaged in the activity.

Austin had difficulty playing cooperatively with others and behavior was the major parent concern.

Austin was uncooperative and showed a lack of interest in all tasks.

Austin was not overly cooperative and he ignored all requests to participate in the testing tasks.

Austin would not come to the table and was uncooperative when presented with a direct request.

Attempted Issues

An early childhood report will certainly want to include a discussion of the tasks the child attempted to perform.

Examples of Attempted Issues

Shelly did not attempt any tasks and no formal assessments were completed.

Shelly would not attempt any tasks when direct requests were made of her.

Shelly attempted all of the tasks presented to her and put forth a good effort during the testing.

Shelly enjoyed drawing and attempted all tasks related to making marks on a paper.

Shelly attempted motor tasks, but seemed to have poor safety awareness during many of the tasks.

Shelly attempted to climb on the table with very little thought about safety or danger.

Shelly did not play with toys, but attempted to mouth toys when they were handed to her.

Comprehension Issues

Early childhood reports often describe the child's ability level and focus on comprehension and how the child understands concepts.

Examples of Comprehension Issues

Mick's delays were characterized by limited comprehension and use of vocabulary concepts.

Mick answered a few questions in the assessment and displayed adequate comprehension with his answers.

There were comprehension concerns as Mick did not understand requests in English or Spanish.

Mick's ability to comprehend language is less than what is expected for his chronological age.

Mick had a blank stare as if he did not comprehend the activity.

Mick had comprehension difficulties as he did not consistently understand or respond to directions.

Mick guessed some of his answers and the school psychologist was unsure if he understood or comprehended many tasks.

Direction Issues

The report can provide a description of how the child follows directions and the child's reaction to receiving a direction.

Examples of Direction Issues

Mike demonstrates the ability to follow routine directions, but sometimes would echo the direction given to him.

Mike easily followed a one-step direction, but had more difficulty with two and three step directions.

Mike was able to follow familiar directions if a gesture was provided with the verbal request.

Mike was cooperative and able to follow simple directions.

Mike disregards directions given to him and often needs directions repeated.

Mike followed directions easily and quickly completed all tasks.

Mike didn't follow directions at first, but took redirection well and completed most tasks.

Demonstration Issues

An early childhood report can describe what a child demonstrates that he or she can do in the assessment.

Examples of Demonstration Issues

Ron can demonstrate action words like sleeping or eating.

Ron demonstrated the ability to pay attention for long periods of time during the assessment.

Ron can replicate block designs from a demonstration.

Ron is still learning to copy a design from a demonstration or written model.

Ron is demonstrating independence during transitions as he moves in and out of his stroller.

Ron demonstrates the ability to pick up objects off of the floor.

Ron was able to demonstrate self-directed play in the preschool setting.

Habit Issues

The report can mention habits, past habits or a history of habit forming behaviors exhibited by the child.

Examples of Habit Issues

Brock's mother indicated he has a habit of overstuffing food in his mouth.

Brock has a habit of eating food very quickly and his father is concerned as he sometimes chokes on food.

Brock has a habit where he paces back and forth and often appears restless.

Brock has an unusual sensory habit where he smells all of the toys before he plays with them.

Brock has a habit of chewing on his clothing and appears anxious.

Brock had a strange habit of constantly pinching other people around him.

Brock has a nervous habit of biting his nails and constantly putting his fingers in his mouth.

Exchange Issues

The report can describe ways a child may be involved in or lack the ability to make exchanges with other child.

Examples of Exchange Issues

Bryce has the skill to exchange social interaction during games and activities.

Bryce is still learning to share and understand give and take situations with other children.

Bryce was observed to take turns with other children in non-verbal exchanges.

Bryce was observed to use the social exchange of 'thank you' several times during the assessment.

No social exchanges were observed during Bryce's assessment and he appeared withdrawn.

Bryce did not understand how to throw the ball back and forth in a throwing exchange with another person.

Bryce does not have an understanding of how to exchange and share toys with other children.

Assistance Issues

An early childhood report can focus on areas where a child may need assistance or how to accommodate a child who needs assistance.

Examples of Assistance Issues

Tom needs assistance for all dressing tasks and he is diapered.

Tom puts many objects in his mouth and will need assistance when playing with toys.

Tom has a tendency to gag on food and will need assistance and supervision when eating.

Tom will need assistance on stairs as he lacks safety awareness.

Tom runs into traffic and will need assistance and supervision as he takes off when on the sidewalk.

Tom falls frequently as he has awkward and uncoordinated movements and will need assistance during outdoor play activities.

Tom needs assistance, supervision and adaptive equipment to support the goals of the preschool classroom.

Delay Issues

The report may describe delay issues and the information can be used to determine special education eligibility and for planning future educational goals.

Examples of Delay Issues

Juan's use of language in social contexts is delayed and should be addressed in the preschool setting.

Results of Juan's assessment indicated a significant delay in the area of expressive communication.

Juan's motor delays have a significant impact on his ability to access the preschool class and elementary school environment.

Juan's scores indicated he is in the very delayed range in the area of daily living skills.

Juan has a mild delay in his socialization skills, but appears to be making progress from early intervention services.

Juan has global delays in all areas and will need a structured learning environment for preschool.

Juan's speech assessment was not completed due to his language delay.

RECOMMENDED READING
for
Report Writing

Peterson, S. (2015). *Autism Report Writing*

Written autism reports contain very important elements in guiding decisions for young children related to autism educational eligibilities and educational placements. **Susan Louise Peterson**, award winning autism author and school psychologist helps professionals look at examples of writing and optional writing formats for phrasing autism reports. *Autism Report Writing* covers writing about initial autism concerns and referrals as well as input from parents and teachers. *Autism Report Writing* also includes ideas about autism behavior, understanding, communication, social, compliance issues and toleration responses. The book ends with ideas for writing recommendations in autism reports. The goal of *Autism Report Writing* is to help professionals write autism reports that give a clear description of the child and his or her complex nature.

Index

A

Ability, 6

Age appropriate, 85

Agency, 45

Alertness, 39

Answering, 15

Anxiety, 44

Assessment, 51

Assistance, 98

Attempted, 92

At-risk, 61-80

Atypical, 34

Avoidance, 53

Awareness, 13

B

Background, 76

Behavior, 5

Birth, 77

C

Change, 83

Child-parent, 29

Communication, 3

Compliance, 32

Comprehension, 93

Consultation, 90

Cooperation, 91

Concern (s), 61-80

Consistent, 38

D

Delay (s), 99

Dental, 80

Dependent, 36

Demonstration, 95

Description, 47

Developmental, 78

Difficult, 33

Direction, 94

Dressing, 74

E

Early childhood, 1

Eating, 71

Effort, 84

Emerging, 82

Emotional, 16

Engagement, 4

Exchange, 97

Experience, 48

Expression, 56, 86

F

Facial, 56

Factors, 41-60

Family, 64

Frustration, 54

Functional, 35

H

Habit, 96

Health, 57

Hearing, 69

I

Illness, 43

Impact, 81-99

Inconsistent, 7

Indication, 40

Initiation, 9

Intensive, 9

Interest, 8

Issue (s), 81-99

L

Language, 19

Learning, 67

Limitation (s), 88

Location, 20

M

Medical, 72

Monitoring, 50

Motor, 70

N

Nonverbal, 24

O

Observation (s), 1-20

P

Participation, 58

Performance, 46

Physical, 18

Play, 12

Pragmatic, 75

R

Redirection, 11

Reluctant, 14

Requesting, 10

Restless, 27

Response (s), 17, 21-40

S

Safety, 66

Self, 87

Sensory, 28

Service, 45

Strength, 60

Struggle, 55

Surgery, 73

T

Tantrum, 25

Testing, 1-20, 49

Time, 37

U

Uncertain, 30

Undetermined, 52

Unstable, 65

Unusual, 31

V

Verbal, 23

Vision, 68

W

Weakness, 59

Withdrawn, 26

Writing, 41

Afterword

Having had the wonderful experience of writing thousands of early childhood reports there is some standard language that tends to repeat itself at times. There are other times reports are redundant as different professionals describe the same characteristics and behavior of the child. However, the best way a professional can write an early childhood report is to personalize the report to describe the child's personal situation, needs, abilities and skills. This will include looking at both the child's strengths and weaknesses along with some emerging skills in the report. **Early Childhood Report Writing** is an important part of establishing the child's first assessment experiences and begins the foundation of describing the child for special education eligibilities, social service recommendations and any assistance the child may need or not need in the educational setting.

www.ingramcontent.com/pod-product-compliance
Lightning Source LLC
Chambersburg PA
CBHW021131300426
44113CB00006B/373